Leader's Guide
for group study of

Be
Daring

Warren W.
Wiersbe

Leader's Guide prepared by
CAROL URIDIL

Six Multiuse Transparency Masters (for visual aids) are included in a removable center section. Instructions for using the Multiuse Transparency Masters are on pages 4-5.

Second printing, 1989

VICTOR BOOKS®
A DIVISION OF SCRIPTURE PRESS PUBLICATIONS INC.
USA CANADA ENGLAND

ISBN: 0-89693-448-9
© 1988 by SP Publications, Inc. All rights reserved
Printed in the United States of America

VICTOR BOOKS
A division of SP Publications, Inc.
Wheaton, Illinois 60187

General Preparation

Before you tear into this leader's guide in all the excitement of preparing for session 1, take time to read pages 3-6.

If you are a little unsure of yourself because you're leading a group of adults for the first time, then follow the simple steps of FOCUS, DISCOVER, RESPOND outlined for each session.

FOCUS will arouse interest and focus your group's attention on the session topic. DISCOVER dynamically involves your group so that they can discover God's truth and its implications for their lives. RESPOND helps group members apply God's truth to their lives.

Even if you're a "veteran" adult group leader who has led multitudes in studies such as this before, this leader's guide can also help you. Simply skim the text for each session and choose the basic lesson parts that will aid you in your personal strategy.

Back to Basics

Read the entire text and this leader's guide. Underline important passages in the text and make notes as ideas come to you. Note any activities in the guide that take advance planning or preparation.

As leader, your enthusiasm for the subject and your personal interest in those you lead, will in large measure determine the interest and response of your group.

Plan to use teaching aids such as a chalkboard or an overhead projector during each session. If neither of these tools is available, use a magic marker on large sheets of newsprint.

Encourage group members to bring their Bibles to each session and use them. It is good to have several modern-speech translations on hand for purposes of comparison.

Getting Started Right

Start on time. This is especially important for the first session because it will set the pattern for the rest of the course.

Begin with prayer, asking the Holy Spirit to open hearts and minds and to give understanding so that the truth will be applied.

Involve everyone. Group involvement is a key to learning. As learners, we retain only 10% of what we hear, 20% of what we see, 65% of what we hear and see, BUT 90% of what we hear, see, and do.

Promote a relaxed environment. Arrange your chairs in a circle or semicircle. This promotes eye contact among members and encourages more dynamic discussion. Be relaxed in your own attitude and manner. As leader, address people by name to help others get acquainted.

Adapting the Course

This material is designed for quarterly use on a weekly basis, but it may be readily adapted to different uses. To use the course over a 12- to 13-week period, simply follow the lesson arrangement as it is given in this guide. Combine sessions if you have fewer weeks in which to cover the material. In some ways, this guide is like a smorgasbord of teaching ideas. As leader, *you* must pick and choose those activities in each session that will best satisfy the spiritual needs of your group members. You can't possibly expect them to digest it all!

A Final Word

Be motivated to master your subject so that you can be the kind of teacher Solomon describes in Ecclesiastes 12:10: *For the Preacher was not only a wise man, but a good teacher; he not only taught what he knew to the people, but taught them in an interesting manner (The Living Bible,* © 1971, Tyndale House Publishers).

MTM Instructions

"What's an MTM?" you ask. It's a Multiuse Transparency Master. Several MTMs are provided for you in the removable center section of this guide; MTMs are designed to increase your teaching impact.

The Victor Multiuse Transparency Masters in this guide will help you enliven your sessions and transmit vital information to the mind through the eye-gate, tying in with educators' recognition of the teaching value of visual aids. They are numbered consecutively (MTM-1—MTM-10) and show with what sessions they should be used. The guide gives specific directions for when and how to use each MTM in the lesson material.

Mechanics

Remove the center section of this guide by opening up the staples in the center. Lift the illustration sheets out and then close the staples again to keep the remaining portion of the guide together. To protect and flatten the MTMs, store them in a regular file folder.

Making Transparencies

You can make your own overhead transparencies inexpensively through the use of these transparency masters. This can be done in at least three ways:

1. *Thermal copier* (an infrared heat transfer process). This is probably the fastest way to make a transparency. Follow the instructions that come with the

copier equipment. Note that the color portions of the MTM are designed *not* to reproduce.

2. *Electrostatic process* (such as Xerox). Make sure that you use the correct film for the right machine. Some color on the MTM will come out gray. On certain MTMs some information, printed in a special light color, will *not* reproduce on machine-made transparencies. This gives you extra information to share orally or to fill in during the session.

3. *Trace your own MTM.* With minimum artistic ability, you can place a sheet of transparent film over the MTM and trace the major parts of the illustration. Exactness is not necessary. For best results, use clear 8½ x 11 sheets of polyester or mylar film (acetate works, but curls). By tracing your own transparencies, you add to your teaching options by being able to make overlays which can be used in a progressive, visually effective way.

Other Uses of Transparency Masters

1. *Visuals.* For small groups, use the MTMs just as they are, as printed visual aids. Or, if you put the MTMs inside clear "report covers," you can write on them.

2. *Spirit masters or mimeo stencils.* From these masters or stencils you can run off material for each group member. Both of these can be made on a 3M Thermofax copier.

Materials Resources

Check with an art supply store for materials such as fiber-tip transparency pens and polyester or mylar film sheets.

A number of distributors carry hundreds of products that can help to make your teaching more effective and fun—for you and your group. If an art store can't supply your needs, try one of these distributors:

Dick Blick Co., Box 1267, Galesburg, IL 61401 ● 309/343-6181; or 215/965-6051 (East Coast); or 702/451-7662 (West Coast).

Faith Venture Visuals, Inc., 510 East Main St., Lititz, PA 17543 ● 717/626-8503.

Nasco Arts & Crafts, 901 Janesville Ave., Fort Atkinson, WI 53538 ● 414/563-2446; or *Nasco West,* 1524 Princeton Ave., Modesto, CA 95352 ● 209/529-6957.

God Opens the Doors

TEXT, CHAPTER 1

A QUICK LOOK

Session Topic Christ will open doors for sharing the Gospel for those who dare to reach out and knock.

Session Goals You will help group members:
1. Come up with synonyms for the phrase "be daring" *(Focus)*.
2. Identify and explain the four key principles which guided Paul's first missionary journey *(Discover)*.
3. Discuss ways to live out the Great Commission in their own lives *(Respond)*.

GETTING READY

What You'll Need
Bibles
Extra copies of *Be Daring*
Map outlining Paul's first missionary journey
Copies of MTM-1
VS-1
Chalkboard and chalk
Pencils and paper
Thesaurus and dictionary
Refreshments

Getting Ready to Teach
1. Distribute copies of *Be Daring* to group members and ask them to read chapter 1 and Acts 13 and 14.
2. Take time to review the text and its basic theme. Read chapter 1 of the book and Acts 13 and 14. Underline important points in the first chapter.
3. Find a map or a set of maps which outline Paul's

journeys. Your pastor or a local Christian bookstore can help you locate this reference material.

4. Make copies of MTM-1 to hand out during the Respond portion of the session.
5. Look over VS-1 and be ready to reproduce it on the chalkboard.
6. Prepare and bring refreshments.

THE LESSON

FOCUS

1. Before the group arrives create an informal atmosphere by having refreshments available. Be sure to welcome everyone and introduce members to each other.

2. Begin the meeting by asking group members to identify synonyms for the phrase "be daring." Try to get everyone to participate. Write down all of their ideas on the chalkboard. (It may be helpful to refer to a dictionary or thesaurus for additional ideas.)

3. Hand out pencils and paper. Ask group members to divide their papers into two columns. In one column have them write: "What being daring meant to Paul," and in the other column, "What being daring means to me." Suggest that they keep these papers in their books, adding points to each side as they progress through this study of Paul's ministry.

DISCOVER

1. Talk about how being daring enabled Paul to take the Gospel throughout the known world. Trace his first missionary journey on the map. Ask volunteers to briefly discuss the highlights of Paul's outreach in the six major cities he visited. If necessary, tell your volunteers to refer to the first chapter of the text. (Try to bring out the following points in the discussion of these cities.)

☐ *Antioch in Syria*—The center of ministry where Barnabas, Simeon, Lucius, Manaen, and Saul (Paul) helped lay the foundations of the church.

☐ *Paphos*—Where the conversion of the Roman official Sergius Paulus took place.

☐ *Perga*—Where John Mark left Paul and Barnabas and returned to Jerusalem.

☐ *Antioch in Pisidia*—Where Paul's three-part sermon reached both Jews and Gentiles.

☐ *Iconium*—Where a multitude of Jews and Gentiles believed, but unbelieving Jews rebelled.

☐ *Lystra*—Where Paul healed the crippled and the people continued to honor false gods despite Paul's message against such practices. Paul is stoned.

2. Draw VS-1 on the chalkboard. Ask group members to identify the four key principles of Paul's first journey. As each point is mentioned fill in the four points of the key. The group should recognize these points:

☐ Paul worked in major cities.
☐ Paul used different approaches for different groups.
☐ Paul emphasized and established local churches.
☐ Paul grounded people in the Word.

Discuss how these principles helped open doors for spreading the Gospel.

3. Ask the group to identify and explain the significance of the three parts of Paul's sermon as revealed in Acts 13:16-42.

4. Review the four important ministries Paul was involved in on his return to Antioch. Suggest that group members refer back to the text or Acts 14:21-28 to find the following ministries:

☐ Preached the Gospel and made disciples.
☐ Strengthened and encouraged believers.
☐ Organized churches.
☐ Reported and shared what was happening.

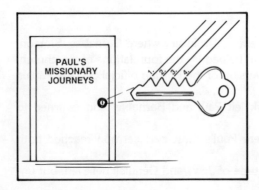

VS-1
List the four key points that opened the door to Paul's missionary journeys.

RESPOND

1. Hand out copies of MTM-1.

2. Give group members a few minutes to read the verses, then ask: **What is the significance of these verses?** Someone should identify them as the "Great Commission." Ask: **How did Paul follow through on these commandments in his first journey?** Direct group members to the text and corresponding Scripture to look for examples.

3. Ask group members to spend a few minutes silently reflecting on ways they might *daringly* enact this commission in their lives.

4. Suggest that they display these verses in a prominent place to remind and motivate them to act.

5. Hand out another sheet of paper to each person. Ask group members to do a comparison of the life of Paul and the life of Christ. Instruct them to keep a list of as many parallels between Paul and Christ as they can find.

6. Close in prayer, asking that the Lord provide each person with courage to be daring for Christ.

ASSIGNMENT

1. Ask members to read chapter 2 of the text and Acts 15:1-35.

2. Encourage group members to record ways in which Paul's ministry showed that he was daring.

3. Challenge group members to find new ways of expressing or sharing their faith.

4. Direct members to the Gospels to locate parallels between the life of Paul and the life of Christ.

5. Request that members come to the next meeting with examples of incidents or experiences that happen during the coming week which involve closed doors and/or compromise.

Don't Close the Doors!

TEXT, CHAPTER 2

A QUICK LOOK

Session Topic   Differences, disputes, and problems can be either opportunities for growth or temptations for division and
dissension.

Session Goals   You will help group members:
1. Brainstorm various "closed-mind" and "compromise" situations *(Focus)*.
2. Give examples of how Paul used compromise to
promote unity *(Discover)*.
3. Plan ways to handle difficult situations with compromise *(Respond)*.

GETTING READY

What   Bibles
You'll Need   *Be Daring*
                Chalkboard and chalk
                VS-2
                Missionary speaker (optional)

Getting Ready   1. Read chapter 2 in the text and the corresponding
to Teach   Scripture. Underline key ideas of the chapter and
                     note important Bible verses.
                  2. Contact a furloughing missionary and ask for assis-
                     tance in presenting the theme of compromise (es-
                     pecially as it relates to the Jerusalem Conference in
                     Acts 15). Ask the missionary to share some exam-
                     ples from her or his ministry in which it was neces-
                     sary to compromise in order to promote unity. Pro-
                     vide the missionary with a copy of *Be Daring* and

summarize the book briefly. Let your guest know that the discussion will be based on chapter 2 of the text and Acts 15:1-35.

3. Be prepared to draw VS-2 on the chalkboard.

4. Throughout the week be aware of examples of closed-mindedness and/or compromise to share with the group.

THE LESSON _____

=========================== **FOCUS** ===========================

1. Begin the session with a time of open prayer. Encourage individuals to *dare* to speak up, share requests, needs, thanks, etc. Close the prayertime asking God to use this session to produce more openness.

2. Ask for volunteers to share "closed-mind" situations they encountered, or became aware of, during the previous week. Then ask them to describe "compromise" situations that they encountered during the past week. Be ready to add your own findings when the discussion slows down.

3. As a group, spend several minutes discussing how a few of the "closed-mind" situations could have been worked out with a unifying compromise.

4. Ask members to identify any situations that have no workable compromise and state the reasons why.

=========================== **DISCOVER** ===========================

1. Ask a couple of volunteers to read Acts 15:1-35 aloud. Have each person read half.

2. Ask: **What was the dispute about in Acts 15?** Be sure that someone brings up these ideas: The legalists were mixing law and grace and rebuilding the wall (removed by Christ) between the Jews and Gentiles by insisting that circumcision and obedience to the law of Moses was necessary for Gentiles to be saved.

3. Write the following formula on the chalkboard:

GOD'S GRACE + FAITH (in Christ) = SALVATION

Ask group members to explain why this formula for salvation, which Paul taught, caused so much division and confusion.

After volunteers share their answers, ask the group to review the reasons Peter, Paul, and James gave for allowing the Gentiles to be part of the kingdom. Direct the discussion in such a way as to include the following ideas:

☐ *Peter* spoke about the past, stating that God had allowed the Gospel to be preached to the Gentiles and had given them the Holy Spirit, thus erasing the difference between Jews and Gentiles through the work of Jesus Christ who removed the yoke of the law.

☐ *Paul and Barnabas* spoke about the present, describing what God was doing (through grace and faith) among the Gentile believers. The miracles that were being performed were proof that God was working with them.

☐ *James* spoke about the future, expressing agreement with Peter and Paul and mentioning that Peter and Paul were in agreement with the Old Testament prophets.

Expand the discussion by asking: **How was a decision made and what was decided by the Jerusalem Council?** Make sure that members understand that with the help of the Holy Spirit the church leaders made a twofold doctrinal and practical decision. They stated that both Jews and Gentiles are saved *only* by faith in Jesus Christ (doctrinal aspect) and that both groups should avoid idolatry and immorality (practical implications).

Ask: **What three things did this decision accomplish?** Make sure the following ideas are brought out:

☐ It strengthened unity, preventing the establishment of extremist "law" or "grace" groups.

☐ It made it possible for the church to witness to lost Jews.

☐ It brought strength to and increased the ministry of the church as the letter announcing the decision was shared in the various communities of the church.

Finally, ask the group to reflect on how this decision was both a meaningful and good compromise.

4. Introduce your guest missionary. Tell the group you invited this

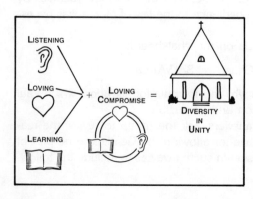

VS-2
Show the formula for effectively spreading the Gospel.

person to share the importance and value of compromise on the mission field. Give the missionary time to speak. Afterward allow time for group members to ask questions.

=============================== RESPOND ===============================

1. Draw VS-2 on the chalkboard. Then read the following lines from Wiersbe's book. "Unity is not uniformity, for unity is based on love and not law. There is a great need in the church for diversity in unity." Ask for group members' interpretation of this concept. Encourage participation by stating that there are numerous interpretations. Direct the group to Ephesians 4:1-17 for help.

2. Give group members time to come up with ways to handle some of their difficult situations with loving compromise. It may be helpful if individuals share problems and get the input of others.

3. Encourage group members to concentrate on two areas: keeping doors open to relationships and sharing the Gospel by remaining open to others.

=============================== ASSIGNMENT ===============================

1. Ask group members to read chapter 3 and Acts 15:36–16:40.

2. Suggest that group members pray for an attitude of loving compromise.

3. Request that each member write a one-sentence summary of his or her personal view of evangelism and bring it to the next meeting.

More Open Doors

TEXT, CHAPTER 3

A QUICK LOOK

Session Topic   In all circumstances caring Christians will be looking for effective ways to share the Gospel.

Session Goals   You will help group members:
1. Come up with a statement describing their personal views of evangelism *(Focus)*.
2. Describe the open doors Paul found with his philosophy of evangelism *(Discover)*.
3. Pray for leading and courage in sharing the Gospel with someone in the coming week *(Respond)*.

GETTING READY

What You'll Need
Bibles
Be Daring
Chalkboard and chalk
VS-3
Transparency of MTM-2
Map of Paul's first and second missionary journeys
Overhead projector
Copies of Paul's and Barnabas' philosophies of evangelism

Getting Ready to Teach
1. Read chapter 3 in the text and Acts 15:36–16:40. Underline key ideas of the chapter and note important Bible verses.
2. Be prepared to draw VS-3 on the chalkboard.
3. Prepare slips of paper to hand out to group members. On half of the slips of paper write Paul's name and his philosophy of evangelism: What can people

do for God's work? On the other half write Barnabas' name and his philosophy: What can God's
work do for people?
4. Obtain a map of Paul's first and second missionary
journeys.
5. Prepare an overhead transparency of MTM-2.
6. Think of or locate a story of how a difficulty or a
problem led to an opportunity to witness. Check a
Christian magazine such as *Guideposts* for an example.

THE LESSON _____

===================== FOCUS =====================

1. Begin the meeting by asking group members to share brief statements summarizing their views of evangelism. Give everyone an opportunity to explain the basis for her or his view. Possible responses might
include: a particular Scripture verse; an example someone else has set; or
a direction they feel God has led them.

2. Continue the discussion by asking each person to take one of the
slips of paper you've prepared. Have the "Barnabas" group meet on one
side of the room and the "Pauls" meet on the opposite side.

3. Give the groups time to discuss the views of their particular missionary. Ask each to come up with the rationale behind the philosophy, biblical
support for the philosophy, and advantages and disadvantages of the
philosophy. While the groups compile their ideas, draw VS-3 on the
chalkboard.

4. Regroup after a few minutes and have each side share the rationale

VS-3
Paul and Barnabas had very different philosophies of evangelism. There
were advantages and disadvantages to both and yet both were necessary and important to the Lord's
work.

and biblical basis of its viewpoint and then the advantages and disadvantages of its viewpoint. Ask a volunteer to write these advantages and disadvantages on the appropriate sides of the balances you've drawn on the chalkboard.

5. After both groups have shared ideas, point out that each opinion is right to a degree and each falls short in some areas. However, God used both philosophies to evangelize in different ways.

6. Ask group members to examine the positives and negatives of their own views of evangelism. Emphasize the fact that the unique qualities of each philosophy will enable God to use each one of them to minister in special ways.

DISCOVER

1. Have one group member read Acts 15:36-41 aloud. Then ask the following:

☐ **What problems or obstacles arose prior to Paul's departure on his second journey?** This passage reveals that a disagreement between Paul and Barnabas concerning John (Mark) forced the two to part company and go separate ways.

☐ **How did God use this separation positively?** This separation led to the formation of two missionary teams, Paul and Silas, and Barnabas and John (Mark). God now had two teams who were then able to evangelize a greater area.

2. Display the map of Paul's first and second missionary journeys.

3. Display MTM-2 on the overhead projector to help group members see how the many "negatives" of the second journey helped to redirect Paul and Silas to many new open doors.

4. Ask someone to explain the roles of Timothy and Lydia in helping Paul.

5. Ask: **What do you think kept Paul going through the difficult times he encountered?** Make sure the following points are brought up: prayer, praise, faith, and Paul's view of evangelism (i.e., his ultimate goal). Be sure to include the point that prayer and praise were (and are) powerful weapons in witnessing. Because of them, God shook the foundations of the prisons and opened the prison doors.

RESPOND

1. Review the varied experiences people have when they become Christians. Open up a brief time of sharing personal experiences by telling the group your story. Encourage others to remember and relate how they became Christians. Point out that the same steps were taken by everyone.

2. End the meeting in silent prayer. Ask each person to pray for an open door to share Christ's saving grace with someone during the coming week. Perhaps there is a friend, neighbor, relative, or work associate needing to hear the Good News.

ASSIGNMENT

1. Encourage group members to read chapter 4 and Acts 17.
2. Challenge group members to implement their evangelism philosophies by reaching out to someone during the coming week.
3. Have group members continue to look for parallels or similarities between the lives of Paul and Christ.
4. Ask for four volunteers to help out with a role play for the next meeting.

Responding to God's Word

TEXT, CHAPTER 4

A QUICK LOOK

Session Topic   Though some will respond negatively to the Good News, it must be remembered that one soul is worth the whole world.

Session Goals   You will help group members:
1. Identify and share typical responses Christians get when sharing the Gospel *(Focus)*.
2. Examine the responses Paul received as he shared the Gospel in Thessalonica, Berea, and Athens *(Discover)*.
3. Discuss and refine their approaches to witnessing *(Respond)*.

GETTING READY

What You'll Need   Bibles
Be Daring
VS-4
Transparency of MTM-3
Overhead projector
Map of Paul's second missionary journey

Getting Ready to Teach   1. Get together with your four volunteers and discuss four different responses that are frequently received when sharing the Gospel. Some possibilities include: rejection, curiosity, interest, and apathy. Assign each person to represent one of these responses (or others that you decide on). Give each of them a list of the questions found in the Focus section and tell them to prepare likely answers for

each question.
2. Read chapter 4 in the text and Acts 17.
3. Prepare an overhead transparency of MTM-3.
4. Be prepared to draw VS-4 on the chalkboard.
5. Try to follow through on last session's witnessing assignment and be prepared to share the response you received.
6. Have a map outlining Paul's second missionary journey to show to the group.

THE LESSON _____

FOCUS

1. Open the session by having the four volunteers sit in front of the group. Introduce them as four potential Christians.

2. Hand out the following questions to various group members:

☐ What do you believe about an afterlife? Heaven and hell?
☐ Are you satisfied with your life the way it is now?
☐ Who do you think Jesus Christ is?
☐ In your opinion, what is sin?
☐ Do you feel a need to be forgiven?
☐ How do you deal with problems, difficulties, and suffering in life?
☐ Do you believe in God? If so, do you think God loves everyone?
☐ What do you think it means to be a Christian?
☐ Can you summarize the theme of the Bible?

3. Give each of the four volunteers an opportunity to answer all of these questions the way the person he or she represents might. Then ask the

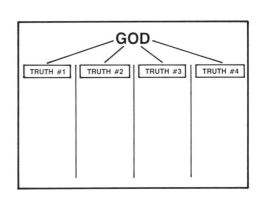

VS-4
List the four basic truths about
God and how these truths are relevant
to all people.

group members to try to identify what kind of response each volunteer represents.

4. Next have group members share the types of responses they received as they witnessed the past week. There should be a variety of responses. Be willing to share the outcome of your witnessing also.

DISCOVER

1. Refer the group to Acts 17 and ask for three members to read this chapter aloud. Divide the chapter as follows: verses 1-9, 10-15, 16-34.

2. Discuss with the group the responses Paul received in Thessalonica, Berea, and Athens. Make sure the following points are brought up.

□ *Thessalonica*. People resisted the Word despite Paul's approach which included: reasoning (questions and answers); explaining Scripture (proving Jesus Christ was the Messiah); and announcing Christ's resurrection.

□ *Berea*. The people received the Word as well as studied, discussed, and tested it.

□ *Athens*. The philosophers and others ridiculed the Word because they were so caught up in idolatry and mythology that their main concern was with enduring or enjoying life.

3. Display MTM-3 on the overhead projector. Have group members relate the responses in these three cities (depicted in the drawings) to some typical twentieth-century reactions to the Gospel.

4. Bring up the author's point that the success of Paul's ministry can be attributed to the fact that he explained God and Christianity by beginning wherever people were spiritually.

5. Ask group members to identify the four basic truths about God that Paul shared with the people of Athens. The group should bring up the following points:

□ The greatness of God.
□ The goodness of God.
□ The government of God.
□ The grace of God.

Draw VS-4 on the chalkboard. Discuss with the group why these four truths are basic to everyone and a good place to start explaining the Gospel. Summarize the group's ideas under each truth.

6. Allow individuals time to identify which of the four truths was most influential in their decision to make a commitment to Christ.

RESPOND

1. Give group members time to share any feelings and inner struggles they encountered when witnessing. This discussion should help group

members identify with each other and realize that no one is alone in dealing with awkward situations. Stress the fact that as new opportunities to witness are sought after or turn up, feelings of rejection can be left behind.

2. Allow group members time to think of positive ways to handle rejections. As the group comes up with ideas, list these on the chalkboard. Some possibilities include: prayer, becoming better acquainted with Scripture passages which relate to nonbelievers' questions, and remembering how Paul and others persevered and were able to endure and survive rejection.

3. Read aloud Psalm 23 in unison as a closing encouragement.

========================= ASSIGNMENT =========================

1. Ask group members to read chapter 5 in the book and Acts 18:1-22.

2. Encourage the group to continually seek for new opportunities to spread the Gospel.

3. Have group members pray for one another as they work at becoming more daring for Christ.

It's Always Too Soon to Quit

TEXT, CHAPTER 5

A QUICK LOOK

Session Topic   Walking by faith means seeing or seeking opportunities, even in the midst of oppression.

Session Goals   You will help group members:
1. Define "walking by faith" (*Focus*).
2. Discuss how Paul handled adversity in ways that motivated rather than discouraged him (*Discover*).
3. Find a key theme that will encourage them and their witness—making them more daring witnesses (*Respond*).

GETTING READY

What You'll Need   Bibles
Be Daring
Copies of MTM-4
Map of Paul's second missionary journey
Chalkboard and chalk
Pencils and paper

Getting Ready to Teach
1. Read chapter 5 in *Be Daring* and Acts 18:1-22. Underline or make notes of key ideas and points that you'll want to include in group discussions.
2. Define what "walking by faith" means to you.
3. Prepare copies of MTM-4 to hand out to group members. Fill out your copy of MTM-4 before the session begins.
4. Bring a copy of a map showing Paul's second missionary journey.
5. Pray for the growing desire to "walk by faith" in

your life and in the lives of your group members.

THE LESSON

============ FOCUS ============

1. When all of the group members have arrived begin a discussion aimed at defining and understanding what "walking by faith" actually means. To get the discussion headed in the right direction, start by reading aloud Hebrews 11. Then write the following phrase on the chalkboard:
WALKING BY FAITH MEANS . . .
Ask group members how they would complete this sentence. Encourage group members to find examples from the reading. List members' responses on the chalkboard. Get the participation of the entire group if possible.

2. After an extensive list has been made, divide the group into three or four smaller groups. Give each group the assignment of summarizing the list you've made on the chalkboard into a concise definition of what "walking by faith" means.

3. After a few minutes have each group select a spokesperson to share its definition with the whole group.

4. Then, as a group, decide on one definition to use for this session's discussion. Write that definition alongside the list on the chalkboard. Ask: **Does this definition have implications for quitting, giving up, or turning back?** (NOTE: The group's definition *should* imply that these aren't options for someone who is "walking by faith.")

============ DISCOVER ============

1. Ask for two or three people to share in reading Acts 18:1-22 aloud. Divide the rest of the group in half. Hand out paper and pencils to all group members. Ask one half of the group to keep track of the discouragements Paul encountered and the other half to note the encouragements God provided. Have the readers begin to read while the two groups write down notes.

2. After the reading of Acts 18:1-22 is completed, have members of the two groups get together and compile their notes into one list for each group.

3. Ask a representative of the "discouragements" group to read each of the group's points one at a time, while a spokesperson from the "encouragements" group states God's provision. Do this until all of the entries from both groups have been read and responded to appropriately.

4. As a group, examine Acts 18 for evidence that supports the following

23

statement: **For Paul, "walking by faith" meant seeing opportunities in the midst of opposition.**

5. Suggest that group members read the following Scripture references to find some assurances God has provided: Hebrews 3:5, Isaiah 41:10 and 43:1-7. Group members should be able to pick out some of the following ideas:

☐ God will never leave us or forsake us.
☐ God will strengthen us and uphold us.
☐ God has redeemed us.
☐ We belong to God.
☐ We are precious in God's sight.

Give members an opportunity to recite or read other verses or promises of God that support these same ideas. Suggest that members make notes of those that might be particularly meaningful to them.

=============== **RESPOND** ===============

1. Pass out a copy of MTM-4 to each group member. Give group members time to fill in the blanks with the necessary information or suggest that they take the MTM home and complete it after they've spent some time thinking and researching. Show the group the copy you filled out in preparation for this meeting. Stress the importance of selecting a meaningful verse, promise, and biblical example to use as an inspiration. Suggest that they keep these MTMs in their Bibles, or some other special place, to refer to during difficult times.

2. Read the following quote from the book: "Divine election is one of the greatest encouragements to the preaching of the Gospel." Get a discussion going about this statement using the following questions:

☐ What does this statement mean?
☐ How can divine election be a real source of inspiration, motivation, and perseverance?
☐ What are some Bible verses which would support this quote?

3. With the remaining time, give group members a chance to personalize the meaning of "walking by faith." Suggest that they write their own definitions on the reverse side of MTM-4.

4. Help group members find prayer partners by having group members count off by twos (1, 2, 1, 2, etc.). Give all of the 1s a slip of paper on which to write their names. Collect these slips and give each of the 2s the opportunity to draw one of the names from a hat. These pairs will be the prayer partners for the coming week.

5. Give the new prayer partners time to meet briefly and share prayer requests.

ASSIGNMENT

1. Ask group members to read chapter 6 and Acts 18:23–19:41.

2. Suggest that group members set aside a few minutes each day to pray for the specific needs of their prayer partners. Encourage prayer partners to contact each other sometime during the coming week.

3. Tell group members to spend some time filling out MTM-4 and to keep looking for key Bible verses which will help them to endure during difficult times.

Excitement in Ephesus

TEXT, CHAPTER 6

A QUICK LOOK_____

Session Topic   Seeing the church grow with new believers is the most exciting part of witnessing.

Session Goals   You will help group members:
1. List and examine the necessary steps to salvation *(Focus)*.
2. Explain the reasons why Paul's ministry in Ephesus was so exciting *(Discover)*.
3. Identify and prepare to guard against those forces that hinder the church's mission *(Respond)*.

GETTING READY_____

What   Bibles
You'll Need   *Be Daring*
Map of Paul's second and third missionary journeys
Chalkboard and chalk
VS-5
Paper and pencils

Getting Ready   1. Read chapter 6 of the text and Acts 18:23–19:41.
to Teach   Make some notes on Wiersbe's main themes (see the session goals above).
2. Be ready to draw VS-5 on the chalkboard.
3. Spend some time looking for Bible verses that talk about being filled with the Spirit or baptized in the Spirit.
4. Spend some time praying for the members of your group. What are their needs? If you don't know, ask. Let members know that you are praying for them.

Your God,

ciples of all nations,
e of the Father and
Spirit, and teaching
have commanded you.
ou always, to the very

Matthew 28:19-20

on You...

More Op

NEGATIVE CONDITION

Paul and Barnabas
go separate ways

Door closed to
Asia Minor and
Bithynia

Paul was imprisioned
in Philippi

MTM-2 Use with session 3 of *Be Daring*

© 1988 by SP Publications, Inc. Permission granted to purchaser to reproduce this visual for class purposes

Berea

Athens

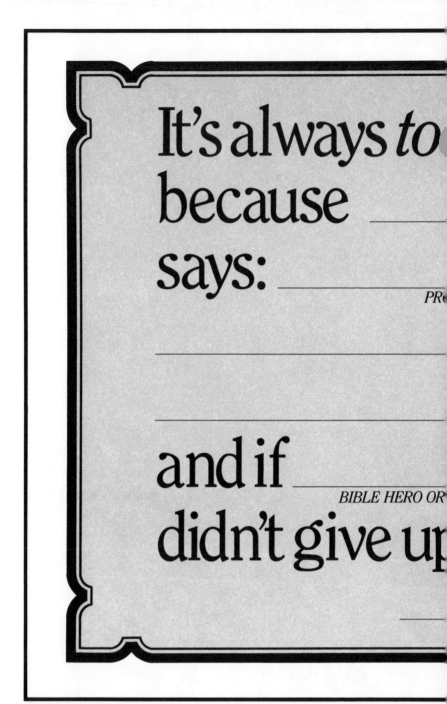

It's always *to*
because _____
says: _____
PR

_____

_____

and if _____
BIBLE HERO OR
didn't give u[

_____

Acts 27: 1-20

1. _____

Acts 27: 21-44

2. _____

MTM-6 Use with session 12 of *Be Daring*
© 1988 by SP Publications, Inc. Permission granted to purchaser to reproduce this visual for class purposes

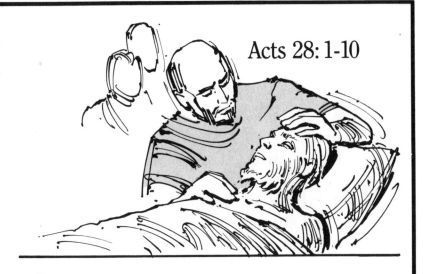

Acts 28: 1-10

3. _____

Acts 28: 11-31

4. _____

- "I lived a Pharisee."
- "I saw a light."
- "I heard a voice."
- "I was not disobedient."
- "I continue
  unto this day."

MTM-5 Use with session 11 of *Be Daring*
© 1988 by SP Publications, Inc. Permission granted to purchaser to reproduce this visual for class purposes

soon to quit

_____
SCRIPTURE VERSE

_____
OR INSTRUCTION

_____

_____,

_____
RACTER

neither will I.

_____
MY NAME

Thessalonica

MTM-3 Use with session 4 of *Be Daring*

n Doors

POSITIVE RESULT

Two missionary teams formed

| Paul and Silas | Barnabas and John (Mark) |

Led west into a new territory — Europe

Prison doors were opened and jailer saved

I, the Lord

Therefore go and make
baptizing them in the
of the Son and of the F
them to obey everythin
And surely I will be wi
end of the age.

Commis

MTM-1 Use with session 1 of *Be Daring*

THE LESSON _____

══════════════════ FOCUS ══════════════════

1. Begin the session by having a brief discussion aimed at answering these questions:
   ☐ **What are the necessary steps to salvation?**
   ☐ **What is the significance of each step?**

2. Draw VS-5 on the chalkboard and fill in the footprints in the order that each step is taken. Have someone read Acts 10:43-48 if necessary. Make sure the group understands these three steps:
   ☐ Hearing the Word.
   ☐ Believing in Jesus Christ.
   ☐ Receiving the Holy Spirit.

3. Ask different group members to express, in their own words, what it means to receive the Spirit. Then, as a group, spend a few minutes looking up and reading Scripture verses on this topic. Some possible verses include: Acts 2:38; Romans 6:3; 1 Corinthians 12:13; Galatians 3:27-29; Colossians 2:11-15; Titus 3:4-5; 1 Peter 3:21. Check a Bible concordance or topical index for other references.

4. Ask: **Why is it exciting to see someone walk the path to salvation? Which step toward salvation do your group members feel is the most difficult to take or accept? Why?** Be willing to share your own opinions and the reasons why you feel the way you do.

══════════════════ DISCOVER ══════════════════

1. Ask members to recall the four different groups, mentioned in the text, that Paul encountered during his three years as a missionary in Ephesus. They should be able to identify:

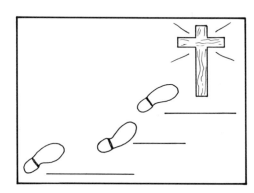

VS-5
Identify the three necessary steps
to salvation.

☐ A man with an incomplete message (*Acts 18:23-28*).
☐ Twelve men with an inconsistent witness (*Acts 19:1-10*).
☐ Seven men with inadequate power (*Acts 19:11-20*).
☐ A mob of indignant citizens (*Acts 19:21-41*).

2. Next divide the group into four smaller study groups and assign one of the four groups Paul encountered to each study group. Tell the study groups that they should review the Scripture verses regarding their assigned group as well as the author's comments in the text. Then hand out paper and pencils and instruct each study group to answer the following questions:

☐ How did Paul come upon this person/group?
☐ What were the flaws in his/their beliefs?
☐ In what ways did Paul minister to this person/group?
☐ What was his/their reaction to Paul?
☐ Why was it exciting for Paul to witness in Ephesus?

You may wish to make copies of these questions for each group or write the questions on the chalkboard.

3. After the groups have had enough time to find answers to the questions, ask each group to choose a representative to share its findings.

4. Continue the group discussion by asking the entire group to evaluate how and why the witness of believers and the special miracles added excitement to Paul's ministry in Ephesus. Group members should point out that those who heard the Word eagerly shared their newfound faith. The miracles God enabled Paul to perform helped to show God's power despite the strong hold Satan had in the occult-filled city.

===================== RESPOND =====================

1. Ask: **What is Christianity's greatest foe today? What is the church's biggest stumbling block? What are the average Christian's greatest temptations?**

2. As group members begin to offer their views write the words CHRISTIANITY, CHURCH, and CHRISTIAN across the top of the chalkboard and make a list of the members' ideas under each. (NOTE: The answers to these questions could possibly create a debate situation as members disagree concerning which is actually the number one problem. There are a couple of ways to handle such a situation: ☐ Give disagreeing members an opportunity to express the reason behind their answers. ☐ Bring the discussion back into focus by stating that it's obvious there are numerous problems, but none will get solved [as is evident by what is going on within the group] unless Christians unite and work together.)

3. Redirect the discussion by having group members come up with

ways to best handle some of the forces of evil listed on the chalkboard. Do this by asking the following questions:

☐ How would Paul have handled this situation?
☐ What does the Bible say about this problem?
☐ What are the roots of this evil?

Then ask the group what is or can be exciting about using the Gospel to solve these problems in the twentieth century.

4. Close the meeting with the Lord's Prayer.

ASSIGNMENT

1. Have the group members read chapter 7 of the text and Acts 20. Suggest that they read the Scripture twice, once before reading the chapter and once following it. Mention that it might be helpful if they note key points during these readings.

2. Encourage group members to pray for the enthusiasm to be daring witnesses for Christ.

3. Ask for six volunteers to meet with you before the next session. Request that these six people read chapter 7 of the text prior to getting together.

A Minister's Farewell

TEXT, CHAPTER 7

A QUICK LOOK _____

Session Topic   Paul's main message, "Christ-centeredness," is the
goal for the church in every generation.

Session Goals   You will help group members:
1. Explore what it means to live a Christ-centered life
   (Focus).
2. List and discuss ways in which Paul's ministry re-
   flected his Christ-centeredness *(Discover)*.
3. Determine ways of becoming more Christ-centered
   (Respond).

GETTING READY _____

What   Bibles
You'll Need   *Be Daring*
                    VS-6
                    Chalkboard and chalk
                    Map showing Paul's third journey

Getting Ready   1. Read chapter 7 in the text and Acts 20. Underline
to Teach   or highlight key ideas in both the Bible and the text.
                    2. Get together with your six volunteers and discuss
                       the six graphic pictures of Paul's ministry described
                       by the author. Tell the volunteers that each one of
                       them will be portraying one of these aspects of
                       Paul's ministry. Give them the following verses to
                       read and suggest they come up with costumes or
                       accoutrements that might help group members
                       guess their traits. Mention that the rest of the group
                       will be given only the initials of the traits. □ PTA—

Paul the accountant—Acts 20:24; Philippians 3:7-11. ☐ PTR—Paul the runner—Philippians 3:12-14; 2 Timothy 4:6-8. ☐ PTS—Paul the steward—1 Corinthians 4:2 (NJV). ☐ PTW—Paul the witness—Acts 20:21; 2 Corinthians 2:15-16. ☐ PTH—Paul the herald—Acts 20:25. ☐ PTWM—Paul the watchman—Ezekiel 3:17-20; Acts 20:31.

3. Be prepared to draw VS-6 on the chalkboard.
4. Think of several examples of people (contemporary or historical) who lived Christ-centered lives.
5. Identify the verses in Acts 20 that you feel best summarize Paul's ministry.

THE LESSON

================= FOCUS =================

1. Begin this meeting with a brainstorming session on the meaning of the following statement: **Christ-centeredness is using my body (life) to reflect Christ.**

2. Draw the stick figure shown in VS-6 on the chalkboard. Tell group members to come up with ways they might use various parts of their bodies to reflect Christian ideals. Give the group an example—Christ-centeredness is using my hands to help others. Then draw a line from the hands out to one of the spaces and write hands—helping. Continue this until most or all of the blanks are filled.

3. Next ask a volunteer to go to the chalkboard and circle the key indications of a Christ-centered life. Get the rest of the group's reaction to those choices and add others if necessary. Make sure the group includes

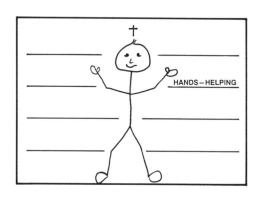

VS-6
Show how we can use our whole lives (bodies) to reflect Christ.

the heart, mind, and soul, which are essential to Christ-centeredness.

4. As a group, come up with a concise definition of Christ-centeredness if possible.

DISCOVER

1. Ask for three volunteers to read Acts 20 aloud.

2. Spend a few minutes looking at the map of Paul's third missionary journey. Be sure to point out the locations of the three farewell events mentioned in chapter 7 of the text: Macedonia, Achaia, and Asia.

3. Summarize this chapter by asking the group to respond to the following questions:

☐ **What was the purpose of this trip?**
☐ **What two goals did Paul have as he visited the churches?**
☐ **What problems did Paul encounter?**
☐ **What miracle did God perform through Paul?**
☐ **What were the three parts to Paul's farewell message?**
☐ **In what way was Paul's message balanced?**
☐ **What kept Paul going—even to the point of dying if need be?**

This last question should bring out the idea that Paul saw himself as a minister of Jesus Christ in all circumstances. When group members hit upon this point, signal your six volunteers to come forward and put on their costumes.

4. Introduce the six volunteers as dimensions of Paul's ministry which enabled him to be an effective missionary. Write the initials PTA, PTR, PTS, PTW, PTH, PTWM on the chalkboard. Then ask group members to try to identify the various dimensions (represented by the initials) and match them with the correct persons, based on the Scripture passages the volunteers read and the actions of the volunteers.

5. Give each volunteer an opportunity to read the corresponding Scripture so group members can then guess what aspect of Paul's ministry each portrays.

6. After all six volunteers have been identified, ask group members to recall examples from Paul's ministry which showed these aspects.

RESPOND

1. Take a few minutes to discuss the content of Paul's farewell message by asking the group to identify some of the dangers "around" us and "among" us.

2. On the chalkboard, list the five dangers (sins) "within" us, which Paul warns about: carelessness, shallowness, covetousness, laziness, and selfishness. Briefly define each sin; then ask group members to share ways

they've been able to avoid these sins. Encourage everyone to listen and learn from each other.

3. Close the session by reading the verses from Acts 20 that you feel best summarize Paul's mission.

ASSIGNMENT

1. Ask group members to read chapter 8 in the text and Acts 21:1–22:29.

2. Ask for two volunteers to come up with a dialog/skit which reveals an unresolved misunderstanding.

The Misunderstood Missionary

TEXT, CHAPTER 8

A QUICK LOOK _____

Session Topic   To be daring for the cause of Christ may result in being misunderstood.

Session Goals   You will help group members:
1. Talk about the truth behind Emerson's statement: "To be great is to be misunderstood" *(Focus)*.
2. Discuss how and why Paul was misunderstood and how he dealt with the consequences *(Discover)*.
3. Prepare to handle situations which may lead to being misunderstood for Christ *(Respond)*.

GETTING READY _____

What   Bibles
You'll Need   *Be Daring*
                    Chalkboard and chalk
                    Map of Paul's third missionary journey and his journey to Rome
                    VS-7
                    Pencils and paper
                    Question sheets *(Discover #1)*

Getting Ready   1. Read chapter 8 in the text and Acts 21:1–22:29.
to Teach   2. Obtain a map of Paul's third missionary journey and his journey to Rome.
                    3. Draw VS-7 on chalkboard.
                    4. Prepare three copies of the following questions about the misunderstandings Paul encountered. Add to these questions any others you feel appropriate. □ What was the misunderstanding about?

□ What was Paul's reaction? □ What did the misunderstanding reveal about Paul? □ What was the final outcome?
5. Pray for group members' awareness of God's faithfulness to those who risk all for Him.
6. Get together with your two volunteers and review their skit.

THE LESSON _____

=============================== FOCUS ===============================

1. After group members have arrived, ask them to think of great people (past or present) whose lives support Emerson's statement: "To be great is to be misunderstood." As members share their examples, ask the following questions of each:

□ **What did this person do which was great?**
□ **Was this person misunderstood in any way? If so, how?**
□ **How did the misunderstanding affect this person? Did it defeat this person or encourage this person to strive harder?**

Is there support for Emerson's statement? Encourage group members to speculate why greatness often results in being misunderstood.

2. Point out that being able to handle misunderstandings positively without creating additional divisions is an ability the truly great frequently possess. This is something Paul often achieved.

3. Spend a few minutes asking volunteers to share some situations in which they were misunderstood. Encourage them to evaluate their handling of the situations. Ask: **Did you handle the situation appropriately?**

QUESTION	PAUL'S FRIENDS	JERUSALEM CHURCH	THE JEWS
1.			
2.			
3.			
4.			

VS-7
Have group members explain the three misunderstandings discussed in chapter 8 of the text.

Looking back, what would you have done differently? Was an understanding ever reached?

=================================== DISCOVER ===================================

1. Divide the group into three smaller groups. Give each group a pencil and a piece of paper, along with a copy of the following questions:

☐ What was the misunderstanding about?
☐ What was Paul's reaction?
☐ What did the misunderstanding reveal about Paul?
☐ What was the final outcome?

2. Assign each group one of the three misunderstandings explained in chapter 8:

☐ Paul's friends misunderstood his plans (21:1-17).
☐ The Jerusalem church misunderstood his message (21:18-26).
☐ The Jews misunderstood Paul's ministry (21:27–22:29).

Ask the three groups to answer the questions as they relate to their assigned topics. Suggest that the groups check the Scripture and that section in chapter 8 of Wiersbe's book.

3. While the three groups work at answering the questions, draw VS-7 on the chalkboard and be ready to fill in the answers to the questions. After the groups have found answers to the questions, ask a spokesperson from each group to share that group's answers while you summarize the responses on the chalkboard.

4. When all the representatives have spoken, discuss with the group how daring Paul was throughout the misunderstandings: in what he said, in what he was willing to suffer, in how he held his ground for Christ. Have group members give examples which relate to each of these areas.

=================================== RESPOND ===================================

1. Ask the two volunteers to come forward and perform their dialog/skit about an unresolved misunderstanding. Tell the rest of the group members to listen and try to come up with ways to resolve the problem portrayed. After the skit ask volunteers to share their solutions.

2. Point out that Christians are frequently misunderstood today just as Paul was. Ask group members to think of some examples where this is true. Brainstorm some ways that Christians can meet these situations head-on, as Paul or Christ might.

3. Point out to the group that Paul and Christ wisely handled situations in different ways, depending on the issues and people involved. Then have group members identify situations Christians should be willing to stand

up to and situations in which Christians might work to promote compromise.

4. Let group members share their ideas on what the Christian's first reaction should be when misunderstood. Ask: **Why is it important for Christians to always press on when misunderstood for Christ's sake?**

5. Close this session with prayer, including any special requests concerning current misunderstandings that need to be resolved.

=========================== ASSIGNMENT ===========================

1. Ask group members to read chapter 9 of the text and Acts 22:30–23:35.

2. Have group members find some well-known biblical promises and bring a list of these Scripture references to the next meeting.

Paul the Prisoner

TEXT, CHAPTER 9

A QUICK LOOK

Session Topic God remains faithful no matter what our circumstances.

Session Goals You will help group members:
1. Explore God's promises to those who believe in Him *(Focus)*.
2. Discuss Paul's attitude while he was a prisoner for Christ *(Discover)*.
3. Find opportunities to demonstrate a greater willingness to serve Christ *(Respond)*.

GETTING READY

What You'll Need Bibles
Be Daring
Chalkboard and chalk
Pieces of paper with Bible verses which tell of God's promises.

Getting Ready to Teach
1. Read chapter 9 in the text and Acts 22:30–23:35. Note important parallels Wiersbe draws between the lives of Christ and Paul.
2. Look up the Bible verses in *Focus #1*. If possible, try to expand the list so that each group member will have two verses to look up. Write each reference on separate slips of paper; then put all the references in a box.
3. Pray for your group members, that they may continue to search for ways to be daring for Christ. Pray for yourself as well.

THE LESSON

FOCUS

1. Before group members arrive, write the following Scripture references (and any other references you can find which express God's promises) on separate pieces of paper: Psalms 37:7; 105:42; Matthew 24:30; Luke 1:54; John 14:3; Acts 1:11; 1 Thessalonians 1:10; 4:16; 2 Thessalonians 1:7; Titus 1:2; Hebrews 10:23; Revelation 1:7. Put the slips of paper in a box and place the box near the doorway or in the center of your meeting table. As group members arrive, have them pick two Scripture references from the box.

2. Tell group members to look up each verse and determine what the promise is and whether the promise has been fulfilled or will be fulfilled in the future. As members look up their verses, make two columns on the chalkboard and title them "FULFILLED" and "FUTURE."

3. Give the group time to look up and categorize their verses before asking them to read the Scripture passages aloud. As group members read their verses, ask a volunteer to write the Scripture references in the appropriate columns on the chalkboard.

4. After all the verses have been read, promises identified, and references listed, ask the following questions:

☐ What purposes do biblical promises serve?
☐ How can knowing these promises strengthen believers?
☐ How did God's promises affect Paul's ministry?

5. Ask group members to share any other biblical promises they remember.

DISCOVER

1. Divide the group into three smaller groups. Assign each group one of the confrontations Paul experienced, as discussed in chapter 9 of the text:

☐ Paul and the Jewish council (22:30–23:10).
☐ Paul and the Lord Jesus (23:11).
☐ Paul and the Jewish conspirators (23:12-35).

2. Have each group reread its topic section in chapter 9 and any related verses. Then write the following questions on the chalkboard and instruct each group to try to answer the questions:

☐ What was the reason for the confrontation?
☐ What was Paul's attitude?

☐ Was the confrontation positive or negative?
☐ What were the results of the confrontation?

Give the group time to research and discuss these questions and any additional questions you want to incorporate. Then ask a representative from each group to share the group's findings.

3. Ask: **What was Paul's attitude toward being imprisoned or cruelly treated? What role do you think Christ's promises to Paul played in helping him remain strong and faithful?**

4. Point out to group members that the author mentions some very interesting parallels in the lives of Paul and Christ in this chapter. Ask them to spend a few minutes reviewing the chapter to locate these insights. Let volunteers share their findings. Some of these insights include:

☐ Both Christ and Paul were in danger from the beginning.
☐ Both suffered at the hands of their own people.
☐ Both Jesus and Paul stood before the Sanhedrin.
☐ Both Christ and Paul were slapped across the face which was illegal and inhumane.

=============================== RESPOND ===============================

1. With the group members input, summarize the courage Paul exhibited in every situation and his firm commitment to his mission goals.

2. Read Matthew 28:20 aloud. Ask: **How can this verse make us more daring for Christ? Why should nothing defeat us? How can you apply this verse daily in your own ministry?** Take time to recite Matthew 28:20 as a group. Then ask group members to recite, from memory if possible, any other verses that express a similar promise.

3. Ask group members to think about new ways they can serve Christ with the kind of willingness Paul displayed throughout his ministry.

4. Close the session with prayer.

============================== ASSIGNMENT ==============================

1. Ask group members to read chapter 10 in the text and Acts 24.

2. Have group members make an effort to continue praying for the group and especially their prayer partners from session 5.

3. Ask for three male volunteers to meet with you sometime during the coming week to help prepare a role play for the next meeting.

Paul the Witness

TEXT, CHAPTER 10

A QUICK LOOK _____

Session Topic The goal of witnessing is to encourage nonbelievers to become believers.

Session Goals You will help group members:
1. Understand why procrastination is Satan's greatest weapon in hindering the spread of the Gospel *(Focus)*.
2. Examine how Paul witnessed to the Roman authorities *(Discover)*.
3. Commit themselves to lifestyles which will encourage nonbelievers to become believers *(Respond)*.

GETTING READY _____

What
You'll Need
Bibles
Be Daring
Chalkboard and chalk
Paper and pencils

Getting Ready
to Teach
1. Read chapter 10 of the text and Acts 24.
2. Make an outline of key points in Acts 24. If necessary, review this chapter in a commentary such as *The Bible Knowledge Commentary, New Testament Edition* (Victor Books).
3. Meet with your three male volunteers and assign each person one of the following personalities to role play: Tertullus, Paul, or Felix. Go over the roles these three personalities played in Acts 24 and 25. Have your volunteers study chapter 10 of the text. Make sure they understand what was going on and

53

why. Have each personality prepare statements which reveal that character's position, role, and beliefs so other group members gain a better understanding of that character's role. If possible, ask volunteers to arrive a few minutes prior to the next meeting to discuss their character portrayals.

4. Write the questions from *Discover #4* on the chalkboard. You may wish to give your three role-play volunteers a copy of these questions to help them prepare for the session.

THE LESSON

FOCUS

1. After group members arrive, ask: **What are some things that people frequently put off doing? What often results from procrastination?** These can be personal areas of procrastination or things commonly put off by many people.

2. Allow time for volunteers to share their ideas. Then ask:

☐ **Why do people procrastinate?**

☐ **If procrastination often has negative results, why do people still put off doing things?**

☐ **Why do nonbelievers often put off a commitment to Christ?**

3. After these questions have been discussed, ask group members to express, in their own words, why procrastination is Satan's most powerful weapon in deterring the spread of the Gospel.

4. Discuss why it is necessary for committed Christians to witness wherever they are, not leaving that responsibility up to someone else. Explain that this too is a form of procrastination that can have eternal consequences.

DISCOVER

1. Ask a volunteer to read Acts 24 aloud.

2. Have your three volunteers take seats in the front of the room and introduce them according to their assigned roles.

3. Let the volunteers begin their personality portrayals one at a time, incorporating as many of the points brought out in chapter 10 as possible.

4. Ask group members to listen carefully with the intent of answering the questions you have written on the chalkboard:

- What were the charges against Paul?
- Why didn't the accusations hold up?
- How did Paul react to the charges?
- In what ways did Paul's answers demonstrate his faithfulness?
- What were the three points of Paul's sermon to Felix and Drusilla? (righteousness, self-control, and judgment to come)
- What is the place of Paul's three points in Christianity?
- How can these points be used to counter Satan's pleas to procrastinate?
- Why do you think Felix and Drusilla ignored Paul's warnings?

RESPOND

1. Ask: Are there ways to encourage nonbelievers not to put off their decision to follow Christ?

2. Give the group members a chance to come up with ways their lives can show that Christianity is appealing, exciting, and worthy of a life-long commitment. Ask them to think of what they would say to someone who asks: "Why should I become a Christian?"

3. Continue the discussion with the following questions:

- What in Paul's life testimony drew unbelievers to Christ?
- What drew you into the Christian faith?
- In what ways can you begin to develop a lifestyle that encourages nonbelievers to follow Christ?
- What in your current lifestyle may discourage nonbelievers from becoming Christians?

Try to get every group member to identify at least one way to encourage non-Christians to live for Christ.

ASSIGNMENT

1. Ask group members to read chapter 11 in the text and Acts 25 and 26.

2. Encourage group members to strive to live lifestyles that make Christianity a reality that others can't and don't want to ignore.

3. Ask group members to choose one of Paul's character traits to become a goal for their own lives.

Paul the Defender

TEXT, CHAPTER 11

A QUICK LOOK

Session Topic   Daring witnesses always defend their faith in Christ.

Session Goals   You will help group members:
1. Discuss the meaning and purpose of defending one's faith in Christ *(Focus)*.
2. Review the five key statements Paul used to summarize his defense *(Discover)*.
3. Come up with a few personal statements which defend their faith *(Respond)*.

GETTING READY

What You'll Need

Bibles
Be Daring
Dictionary
Chalkboard and chalk
Copies of MTM-5
Paper and pencils

Getting Ready to Teach

1. Read chapter 11 of the book and Acts 25 and 26. For more information check a Bible commentary. Note main themes and facts you'll want to bring out during the meeting. Think of ways to relate these themes to your group members' lives.
2. Make copies of MTM-5.
3. Come up with a few statements to defend your faith in Christ. (Note Paul's statements in chapter 11 of the text.)
4. Think of some situations when you were unprepared to defend your faith. Try to recall any awk-

wardness you experienced.

5. Pray that your group members see the necessity of being prepared to courageously defend their faith.

THE LESSON

================ FOCUS ================

1. Begin the session by reading from a dictionary the definition of defend. Then ask: **What does it mean to defend one's faith? When might it be necessary or important to be able to defend one's faith? What are the prerequisites to successfully defend one's faith?**

2. Expand the discussion by telling the group of any instances where you felt poorly prepared to defend the Christian faith. Discuss what you did, what you said, and what kind of impression you made. Allow others to share their experiences.

3. Draw the following conclusion: defending the Christian faith means being able to confidently express what we believe, why we believe, and how these beliefs provide us with eternal rewards that others can also share.

================ DISCOVER ================

1. Briefly review the contents of Acts 25 and 26. Write the following three subheads from the text on the chalkboard:

☐ CONCILIATION: FESTUS AND THE JEWISH LEADERS;
☐ CONSULTATION: FESTUS AND KING AGRIPPA;
☐ CONFRONTATION: FESTUS, AGRIPPA, AND PAUL.

2. Either have volunteers read the Scripture relative to these subheads or begin by asking for volunteers to explain what the conciliation, consultation, and confrontation were about. Write short statements which help to summarize the encounter below each subhead. These summaries should be based on the group's responses to the following questions:

☐ **What did the Jews accuse Paul of?**
☐ **What was the situation between Festus and the Jewish leaders?**
☐ **What did Festus decide?**
☐ **Why did Paul want to appeal to Caesar?**

3. Move the discussion to the meeting between Festus and Agrippa and ask:

☐ **What was Festus' dilemma before consulting Agrippa?**

☐ What did Festus tell the king about Paul?
☐ What did the king say?

4. Hand out copies of MTM-5. Then expand the discussion to the meeting of Festus, Agrippa, and Paul by asking the following questions:

☐ What promise was being fulfilled by this meeting?
☐ How was Paul able to defend himself and witness at the same time?
☐ How would you summarize the significance of Paul's five key statements (I lived a Pharisee; I saw a light; I heard a voice; I was not disobedient; I continue unto this day)?
☐ In what way was Paul the judge and Agrippa and Festus actually the prisoners on trial?
☐ Why do you think the word *witness* is a good summary of Paul's life and ministry?
☐ What were Agrippa's and Festus' replies to Paul's questions?
☐ What was Agrippa's and Festus' final decision? Why did they decide the way they did?

=================== RESPOND ===================

1. Hand out paper and pencils. Tell group members to spend a few minutes thinking about what being a Christian means to them personally. Ask them to write out their best statements. To help them in this task have them think about the following questions:

☐ What were you like before you met Christ?
☐ What changed you?
☐ What do you believe?
☐ Why do you believe?
☐ Why do you continue to believe?

2. After group members have come up with their own ideas, encourage volunteers to share their answers or statements. Be prepared with a set of your own statements to share with the group.
3. Close the session with prayer.

=================== ASSIGNMENT ===================

1. Ask group members to read the last chapter in the text and Acts 27 and 28.
2. Have group members come up with a few words that best describe Paul's life and ministry.

Paul Arrives in Rome

TEXT, CHAPTER 12

A QUICK LOOK

Session Topic   God leads, guards, protects, and delivers believers through the storms of life.

Session Goals   You will help group members:
1. Identify the typical storms that occur during the various stages of life *(Focus)*.
2. Describe the roles Paul played during the storms and shipwreck *(Discover)*.
3. Determine how to best keep the faith in difficult times *(Respond)*.

GETTING READY

What You'll Need

Bibles
Be Daring
Chalkboard and chalk
MTM-6
Map which outlines Paul's voyage to Rome
3 x 5 cards
Paper and pencils

Getting Ready to Teach

1. Read chapter 12 in the text and Acts 27 and 28. Keep a list of the trials Paul endured in Acts 27 and 28 and how he dealt with them.
2. Locate a story or find a person to share a personal story of a trial or a storm where God revealed Himself in some way.
3. Make four copies of the four human reactions listed in *Focus #2*.
4. Make copies of MTM-6.

5. Take time to identify the worst storm in your life. Be willing to share how God delivered you.

THE LESSON

=== FOCUS ===

1. Divide the group into four buzz groups. Try to have both males and females in each buzz group. Hand out pencils and paper and assign one of the following age brackets to each buzz group: childhood, adolescence, adulthood, old age.

2. Have each group spend some time coming up with typical storms (trials) common to those years of life. Ask the groups to try to identify whether or not the storms are the result of one of the following four reactions: impatience; accepting advice that is contrary to God's will; following the majority; trusting ideal conditions.

3. While the groups brainstorm ideas, make four columns on the chalkboard. Head each column with one of the age-groups.

4. When the buzz groups have compiled their lists, ask them to choose a representative to share their ideas. Start with the childhood group and work toward old age. Fill in the columns as the ideas are shared.

5. After each group representative has had an opportunity to speak, allow the entire group to volunteer answers to the following questions:

☐ Which of the four reactions gets people into the most storms?
☐ Are any of the four reactions more common at certain ages?
☐ Which of these four reactions were directly responsible for the storms described in Acts 27 and 28?
☐ What four practical lessons are revealed concerning storms in chapter 12 of the text?

Make sure group members understand the author's main ideas:

☐ *Storms often come when God's will is disobeyed.*
☐ *Storms have a way of revealing character.*
☐ *Even the worst storms cannot hide the face of God.*
☐ *Storms give us the opportunity to serve others and bear witness to Jesus Christ.*

=== DISCOVER ===

1. Hand out copies of MTM-6 and ask group members to identify Paul's role in each of the pictures. Have group members write that role in the space provided. They should identify:

☐ Paul the counselor (27:1-20).
☐ Paul the encourager (27:21-44).
☐ Paul the helper (28:1-10).
☐ Paul the preacher (28:11-31).

2. After the four roles have been identified, ask group members to find as many examples as possible of Paul in each role. If time permits and you wish to expand the discussion, give the group members time to review previous sessions for additional examples. Refer the group members to the appropriate Bible verses to find examples.
3. Ask: **What did these roles teach those Paul was with or spoke to about Christianity? What did Paul's behavior throughout the storms reveal about his faith? What do these two chapters in Acts tell us about God's revelation, will, presence, and power? How did Paul's voyage review the four truths about storms mentioned in Focus?**
4. Have group members share the few words they feel best describe Paul's life. Ask: **How are these ideas visible in Paul's actions and reactions in Acts 27 and 28?**

RESPOND

1. Give group members an opportunity to recall the worst storms in their lives. Let those who are willing share their experiences.
2. Ask: **How can a person keep the faith in times of trouble? What Bible verses can help? What role does prayer play? How can fellowship be an encouragement? What do you do when God seems silent?**
4. Encourage group members to write down new ways to keep the faith when they go through life's storms. Remind them how Paul carried out his commission through storms, shipwrecks, prison, and torture, because he knew that Christ was always with him.
5. Close the session with silent prayer. Encourage group members to pray for the ability and desire to be daring witnesses for Christ.

ASSIGNMENT

1. Ask group members to review all the previous sessions, taking special note of each session's focus and goals. Have them identify the session which was most meaningful for them and write brief statements describing why.
2. Request that group members try to come up with a brief definition that summarizes what "being daring for Christ" means to them.
3. Hand out 3 x 5 cards and instruct group members to list Scripture references which encourage them to "be daring." Suggest they take time to memorize and/or underline these verses in their own Bibles.

Review

TEXT, CHAPTERS 1–12

A QUICK LOOK

Session Topic To "be daring" involves individual choices that change and expand as we grow in faith.

Session Goals You will help group members:
1. Summarize what being daring means to them *(Focus)*.
2. Determine what being daring meant to Paul *(Discover)*.
3. Pray to become more daring for Christ *(Respond)*.

GETTING READY

What You'll Need
Bibles
Be Daring
Chalkboard and chalk
Maps of Paul's missionary journeys and trip to Rome
Refreshments

Getting Ready to Teach
1. Review chapters 1–12 of the text. Come up with your own definitions of what being daring meant to Paul and what it means to you.
2. Finalize your research into the similarities in the lives of Paul and Christ.
3. Decide which areas of your life you need and want to become more daring for Christ. Make a list of these.
4. Pray for the last group meeting. Ask that God would instill a desire within each person to be daring for Him. Pray also for the ability to encourage each other in this lifelong pursuit.

5. Prepare to have refreshments for group members to share together before disbanding and going into all the world.

THE LESSON

FOCUS

1. Share a time of refreshments at the beginning of this last meeting.

2. After everyone has arrived and helped themselves to refreshments, begin an informal meeting by asking members to get out the charts they have been keeping on what being daring means to them. Ask them to share their personal views. Write their ideas on one half of the chalkboard. Add your own ideas when appropriate. Try to encourage the participation of everyone. Each new idea will help deepen the thinking of the entire group. Indicate with a star those concepts that are mentioned more than once.

3. Suggest that group members add any new ideas to their lists as long as the ideas are ways they personally want to become more daring.

DISCOVER

1. Ask group members to describe what being daring meant to Paul. Write their ideas on the other half of the chalkboard.

2. Give members time to share the specific experiences or struggles which reveal Paul's daring qualities. This should be a good review of the text. You may want to ask members to reread the parts of Acts relative to their comments.

3. At this point it may be helpful to retrace on a map Paul's missionary journeys.

4. As a group, attempt to identify Paul's most daring acts and qualities. Note the most daring qualities by placing a star next to them on the chalkboard.

5. Allow group members a few minutes to make a silent comparison between what being daring meant to Paul and their summary definitions of what it means to them. Then as a group, discuss the differences. Use the following questions to spark the discussion:

☐ What enabled Paul to be daring in so many difficult situations?
☐ What was Paul's initial reaction to trouble?
☐ What was Paul's main goal in life?
☐ What role did faith play in Paul's life?
☐ Were Paul's situations any more difficult than those we face?

1. Have group members get out their charts on the parallels between the lives of Paul and Christ. Ask volunteers to share similarities they noticed during the study of *Be Daring*. Share any additional ones you may have found through your research. Discuss these likenesses by asking the following questions:

☐ What do these similarities say about Paul?

☐ What do the lives of Paul and Christ say about dealing with trials and temptations?

☐ What do Paul's and Christ's life say about the power of the Gospel?

☐ What do their examples establish as standards for living the Christian life?

Be sure to point out that the likenesses show Paul's total commitment to the cause of Christ, his love for Christ, and how closely he strove to walk in his Master's footsteps. Paul's example is a great gift. God not only used him to reach the lost, but to serve as an encouraging example for all future generations of Christians.

2. Give group members time to share examples from Paul's life which have motivated them to be more daring. Was there something in particular he said, did, or endured that stands apart from everything else? Have group members share the session that was most meaningful to them.

3. Spend the last few minutes talking about specific ways group members plan to implement a daring lifestyle for Christ—as individuals, as a group, or within the church.

4. Close with a time of open prayer to express concerns, desires, hopes, and a growing willingness to become more daring.